Sheldon Ronningen

D1258393

# 'QUICK TRAINING FOR WAR'

## FIRST REVIEWS, 1914

*Daily Mail.*—"B.P. has a reputation which is second to none, and this little book is so brightly and cleverly written that it will be read with advantage by the recruit and studied with infinite pleasure and profit by the professional soldier."

*Lady's Pictorial.*—"Ladies who are anxious to give a practical present which not one of their soldier men-folk should disdain to accept would certainly find this acceptable."

*Globe.*—"I advise every young officer, Regular or Terrier, to get 'Quick Training for War' and study it.... It is a most sunny and stimulating book."

*Sporting Chronicle.*—"Great interest is being taken in Baden-Powell's book 'Quick Training for War' which is enjoying a tremendous boom."

*Daily Chronicle.*—"The volume is full of good things for every officer, N.C.O., and man in the British Territorial Forces, and rifle club."

*Daily Telegraph.*—"This little handbook should be a companion of all officers and men now training or being trained for war."

*Academy.*—"If books were sold on intrinsic value, Sir Robert Baden-Powell's little volume would be issued at a sovereign."

*Sporting Life.*—"Should be studied by every man who is entering the service of his country or contemplates doing so."

*Spectator.*—"In heartily commending General Baden-Powell's little book to the trainers of the New Army we should like," etc.

*Athenæum.*—"Sir Robert's hundred pages teem with evidence of how common-sense helps."

*Truth.*—"Will prove a valuable gift to those who have answered the appeal of the War Office."

*Sunday Times.*—"The book should be in the knapsack of every recruit in the New Army."

*Daily Express.*—"A copy ought to be in the pocket of every officer and man in the new armies."

*Daily Sketch.*—"Every young officer, N.C.O. and private should have a copy."

*Morning Post.*—"As instructive as it is interesting."

*Saturday Review.*—"A manual of great good sense."

*Daily Graphic.*—"It is concentrated wisdom."

*Observer.*—"Clear and persuasive to a degree."

# QUICK TRAINING FOR WAR
# BY SIR ROBT. BADEN-POWELL

One way is this, but it leaves the work **visible to** the enemy

Another and often preferable way is this

WHAT TO DO WITH BUSH IN FRONT OF DEFENCE WORKS

# QUICK TRAINING FOR WAR

## A FEW PRACTICAL SUGGESTIONS
## ILLUSTRATED BY DIAGRAMS
## BY LIEUT.-GEN.
## SIR ROBERT BADEN-POWELL, K.C.B.

DEDICATED TO THE YOUNG OFFICERS

AND MEN WHO HAVE COME FORWARD

IN THEIR COUNTRY'S DEFENCE

**CONWAY**

**Acknowledgements**

I would like to thank my colleague at the Defence Studies Department, JSCSC, Dr Nick Lloyd and also Professor Peter Simkins, formerly of the Imperial War Museum and now at the Centre for First World War Studies at the University of Birmingham, for their generous help and advice.

**Dr Martin Robson**, Defence Studies Department, King's College London at the Joint Services Command and Staff College, Defence Academy of the UK.

The analysis, opinions and conclusions expressed or implied in this publication are those of the author and do not necessarily represent the views of the JSCSC, the UK MoD, The Corbett Centre for Maritime Policy Studies or King's College London.

Introduction © Martin Robson 2011
Typesetting and layout © Conway 2011

Originally published in 1914 by Herbert Jenkins Limited.

This edition published in the United Kingdom in 2011 by Conway,
An imprint of Anova Books Ltd.
10 Southcombe Street
London W14 0RA

10 9 8 7 6 5 4 3 2 1

A CIP record for this book is available from the British Library.

ISBN 9781844861439

Printed and bound by Grafo, Spain

# FOREWORD

**P**LEASE do not think that this little book is intended as a substitute, in the form of "Potted Tactics", for the excellent training manuals issued by the War Office—because it is not.

The principles contained in these books require to be fully mastered by every officer and N.C.O. who wants to train his men and to gain their confidence, and therefore their obedience, on service.

But the present crisis demands a quicker development of some sort of efficiency for the field than is laid down in those books, and therefore I have attempted to give in the following pages a few suggestions from practical experience to this end, and towards developing that *spirit* which is described in those manuals as the essential part of military training.

Since the men are as keen to learn as the officers are to teach I should be glad if these hints may be found helpful, not only to the officers and N.C.O.'s in training, but also to the men in learning their work as defenders of their country.

ROBERT BADEN-POWELL.

# CONTENTS

# DIAGRAMS

# INTRODUCTION

Lord Robert Baden-Powell's *Quick Training for War* is a book of practical soldiering suggestions produced in response to the outbreak of war in August 1914. At first glance it might seem an anachronism. Yet as with his seminal work *Scouting for Boys* (1908), there is much in *Quick Training* that is of interest for the general reader and historian alike.

If anyone was in a position to write a short, punchy and accessible volume to inform those who flocked to join the British Army in the autumn of 1914 it was probably Baden-Powell. During the Boer War Colonel Baden-Powell's leadership at the defence of Mafeking (October 1899-May 1900) made him a national hero. He even found time during the siege to read the proofs of his 1899 book, *Aids to Scouting*.[1] This work displayed the utility of his thinking – the passing on of lessons learned the hard way for assimilation into the wider 'military experience'. In 1901 Baden-Powell was appointed to raise and train the South African Constabulary, providing him with experience of the practical problems inherent in training. All this he implemented in his well-known scouting programme, culminating in the publication of *Scouting for Boys* in 1908. Coinciding with this work he was consulted by the then Secretary of State for War, Richard Haldane, regarding the raising of a territorial force – 'to take up the training of a force of some forty thousand men to give a system and a standard for others to train on'.[2]

When war came in 1914 the now retired Baden-Powell called at the War Office to offer his services to Field Marshal Lord Kitchener. Kitchener knew the scouting organisation well; he was President of the North London Boy Scouts. Kitchener believed the war would be longer than most people expected and was opposed to the territorial concept – instead he raised a new professional army to reinforce the regulars committed to France. This new army would, of course, require training. Baden-Powell served on the very short lived (4 days!) Midleton Committee which was to help with the coordination of the training of Kitchener's new recruits;[3] clearly he was seen as an important individual within the recruitment debates.

It does not seem, however, that any official sanctioning or guidance was given to Baden-Powell for the creation of *Quick Training*. He certainly wrote it sometime in August and September 1914, for he makes reference to the Belgian defence of Liège (4-16 August). The book went through five editions in September 1914 alone, with over 65,000 copies sold. Affordably priced at one shilling, on 23 September *The Times* Book Club selected it as a 'Book of the Moment', declaring it 'A clear, persuasive, clever little book full of wit and wisdom. It tells the essential things for a soldier, and will make soldiering delightful and successful'.[4]

Along with the desire to share his practical suggestions, such commercial success might also point to another of Baden-Powell's motivations: opportunism. Not just commercial opportunism, although that cannot be ruled out, but also the opportunity for a 57-year old former officer to support his country in time of need. Clearly the success of

*Scouting for Boys* ensured that a book carrying Baden-Powell's name would have a captive market.

In *Quick Training* Baden-Powell's intent is plain right from the start with his dedication of the text to 'the young officers and men who have come forward in their country's defence'; clearly the prime audience was not the regular army, for that had a plethora of manuals in existence; primarily *Infantry Training (4-Company Organisation)* 1914, which stressed fire and movement, rapid weight of rifle fire and small rushes – all tactics drawn from the experience of the Boer War.[5] While it would also serve the needs of the 478,893 men who, between 4 August and 12 September 1914, responded to Kitchener's call by volunteering for the army, Baden-Powell did not think his volume a substitute for the 'excellent training manuals issued by the War Office'. Instead, using his experience of the Boer War, his intended audience was those who had little or no experience of 'soldiering'; in particular the new junior officers and NCOs. In other words, it was for those who needed to display leadership to instil confidence in their men – or as Baden-Powell himself states – 'develop spirit'. Key to Baden Powell's approach were the four 'C-s' of soldiering – courage, common sense, cunning and cheerfulness; along with practical advice for implementation.

This all sounds rather quaint and it is no surprise to find Baden-Powell using the language and norms of his time – he was, after all, the 'Hero of Mafeking', a product of the British Empire. In the late summer and autumn of 1914 there were many who thought the war would be a 'boy's own adventure', 'playing the game' to give the Hun a sound thrashing. One young soldier summed up the feeling: 'we thought this is going to be a short sharp war, quick training, over to France and back again, and finished'.[6] Of course we have the benefit of hindsight, but for those in 1914 looking for pointers to the future character of warfare we must remember that the last major European conflict, the Franco-Prussian War, still had much in common with Napoleonic warfare – a million miles away from what the First World War would become. With this in mind, British official and unofficial military thinkers derived lessons from their recent experience of the Boer War –

a point Baden-Powell makes repeatedly in this book.

It is difficult to judge *Quick Training*'s immediate impact. Despite the large number of copies sold, a search of contemporary diaries and memoirs has failed to throw up any mention of it. We do know that official manuals, booklets and pamphlets were read. Guy Chapman of the 13th Royal Fusiliers recalled 'We seized on and devoured every fragment of practical experience which came our way' including the pamphlets produced at the front called 'Notes from the Front'. A plethora of private publications were produced in the run up to and following the outbreak of war in 1914, such as E. Dane's *Trench Warfare or E. Solano's Field Entrenchments: Spadework for Riflemen.*[7] Baden-Powell's book was one of many publications competing for sales in the market. Certainly, over 65,000 were sold but the question we cannot answer is: to whom? If officers, NCOs and men took them to France, then many might have been lost in the mud of Flanders. Perhaps the main purchasers were scouts themselves, keen to get their hands on the latest Baden-Powell work? Perhaps Baden-Powell's advice was judged irrelevant in 'modern' war once the lessons of the Western Front started to be assimilated in official publications?

Despite the author's quaint anecdotes about meeting Kaiser Wilhelm II or using cavalry to reconnoitre enemy positions, *Quick Training* contains nuggets of enduring relevance. From the importance of small unit morale, combating boredom and maintaining fitness (mental and physical) to the employment of common sense and motivating the men, *Quick Training* focuses on the concerns of the soldier. Hence, at the human as well as the military level, his work remains readable, enjoyable and educational.

Martin Robson, Ide, 2011

[1] *Aids to Scouting for N.C.O.s and Men*, Bt.-Colonel R S S Baden-Powell, FRGS, 5th Dragoon Guards, (Gale & Polden, 1899).

[2] Cited in Hillcourt, W., *Baden-Powell, Two Lives of a Hero*, (Heinemann, 1964), p.275.

[3] Simkins, P., *Kitchener's Army: The Raising of the New Armies, 1914-1916*, (Pen & Sword, 2007), pp.73-75.

[4] *The Times*, Wednesday, 23 September 1914.

[5] *Infantry Training (4-Company Organization) 1914*, (General Staff War Office, 10 August 1914).

[6] Cited in Simkins, p.228.

[7] Bull, S., *An Officer's Manual of the Western Front, 1914-1918*, (Conway, 2009), pp.8-9.

# QUICK TRAINING FOR WAR

## I

### THE MAKING OF AN ARMY

**T**HERE was an argument a short time back as to how long it takes to make an efficient soldier out of the average recruit material, and a patriotic newspaper proved by experiment, what many of us already knew, that it was quite feasible to turn out the finished article in six months under favourable circumstances.

But it may be remembered that immediately before the South African campaign we had to take such material as we could find and turn it out efficient for the field in something nearer six weeks than six months. Men whom we enlisted in

August were fighting, and fighting well, in
October. This was not brought about by
teaching them the goose-step, but rather
by going straight to the point desired and
teaching them to fight in the field. It is
comparatively easy to turn out soldiers,
if, by soldiers, you mean lads who can dress
smartly and march past accurately and
well; but these are not necessarily effective
for the work of fighting battles against a
fighting enemy. Drill is not everything.
If it were the Germans would not lose the
smallest combat, nor would the Boers,
entirely undrilled as they were, have been
able to put up such a good fight as they
did for two years in the South African
campaign.

### THE RAW MATERIAL

One day in Hyde Park recently I watched
for some time the young officers training
their men for the war before us. Memories

of my own subalternhood came vividly back to me. I knew their thoughts and I should like to help them. I saw myself back again with my squad of young soldiers, my pocket bulging with the over-sized drill-book of which I had endeavoured to assimilate a portion by heart, and was then trying to give out to the men. I cannot say I was highly interested in the job—nor were my men. I was probably thinking how my overalls fitted and how soon I might dismiss for breakfast, while I gave periodical parrot-like utterances of extracts from the book.

If only someone who knew could have given me an idea of the inner meaning and the possibilities which underlay the training, what a difference it would have made. How those long, dreary hours of dull routine would have shortened themselves, both theoretically and materially, for myself and my men. It was not until years later that light dawned upon me. I had thought that the letter of the book was the sure fetish to success in war. I never read the meaning which lay between the lines.

### THE INNER MEANING OF DRILL

As regards squad-drill the under-meaning of it is that, while exercising your squad, you should get to know, not merely the name, but the character and the alertness of mind and capabilities of each one of your men. In the meantime each one of these, unconsciously it may be, is also sizing you up. His life is possibly going to be in your hands. When that time comes he is going to behave towards you as he knows you, and you ought to be inculcating that confidence in you which will bind your men to stick to you in a tight place.

I remember an officer who was a bit of a martinet, who, by his cursing and punishing the men, had roused amongst them a thorough hatred for himself; but he was plucky, there was no doubt whatever of that. One morning when ordered on an expedition with his force, he formed the men up and said, "I know you hate me, and you mean to shoot me in the back at the first opportunity. All I advise you is not to do so just yet. We have got a rough time before us to-day, and it wants a bold push. If you stick to me I'll take you through. You can shoot me as much as you like afterwards." Needless to say the enterprise succeeded and he was never shot.

## MUTUAL SIZING UP

The sizing up of your men at squad or any other drill requires a close observation and quick eye. In my subaltern days I was lucky enough to make a success of my very first parade, the day after I joined, and in this wise. My troop was ordered

to parade in double rank, and I was given
by my captain the simple task of walking
round to inspect the men and to see that
each of them was wearing a cholera belt.
Shirts were thrown open and I walked down
the front rank, finding each man dressed as
he should be. As I turned at the end to
come up the rear rank with my eyes down-
cast from sheer shyness at commanding a
parade, I just caught with the tail of my eye
a movement at the opposite end of the troop,
as a man stepped from the rear rank into
the front rank which I had just examined.
I only knew the name of one man in the
troop at that time, because he had been
detailed to bring me my horse, and this hap-
pened to be the man who stepped across. I
took no notice of the move, as I had to debate
in my mind whether or not it might be a bit of
orthodox drill that, when the officer arrived
at the rear rank, one of its number should
step into the front rank. As I passed along

the rear rank examining their belts I pondered the matter over, and came to the conclusion that I would risk matters and call this man out.

On arriving at the front again, I called, "Private Ramsbotham, step to the front. Have you got your cholera belt on?" There was a blushing, confused reply of, "No, sir." I did not punish him, as I was not clear what powers of punishment I had; but I said, with much fear and great gruffness, "Take care you don't allow it to occur again," and dismissed him. But the punishment which he afterwards got from his own comrades in the way of jeers at being caught out by a fresh-joined subaltern was far heavier for him to bear than any that I could have inflicted.

## OFFICERS AND MEN

A subaltern or non-commissioned officer, if he desire to succeed in getting the best out of squad drill, must practise the closest observation on every one of his men.

I have only just received the Defence Force report from one of our Oversea Dominions, which contains these suggestive paragraphs:

"Squadron or company training brings commanders into touch with their subordinates very much to the advantage of both. Here officers and non-commissioned officers learn to make practical application of the knowledge they have acquired at their classes, and become the recognised instructors of men already prepared by their work as recruits to profit by such tuition. Here, by degrees, the captain, subaltern, sergeant, or corporal becomes, each in his own sphere, the recognised leader, guide, enlightener of his men. Here, in short, the commander obtains that ascendency over the minds of the men which engenders discipline.

"But what, after all, is this modern discipline? The men join the ranks full of good will and anxiety to acquit themselves well in the performance of a duty demanded of them by the State. The officers and non-commissioned officers are at least equally anxious to show them how best to achieve this same national purpose. Gradually mutual esteem, and very probably affection, are evolved out of the relationship of eager master and willing pupil. The two are knit together more and more closely by the generous warmth of feeling consequent on working for a purely unselfish object. There is no money in it. If the commander sweats the subordinate, that sort of sweat does not go to make the commander fat. On the contrary, he is bound in honour to sweat himself at least twice as much as his men. The rank and file (the workers) recognise these truths instinctively and very quickly. They learn to trust their instructors, and the instructors learn to trust them. When this point has been reached the unit will bear the

strain of discomfort and danger without any loss
either of cohesion or courage."

THE NECESSITY FOR DRILL

In raising the force now needed for the
defence of the country, we have, if I may
judge from appearances, the best possible
material. The men are eager and willing
to learn. As a friend has expressed it,
"there is in these men's eyes the look that
is sometimes seen in that of a dog when he
seems to say, 'What is it that master wants?
If only I knew!'" And indeed the men
seem eager to learn; but it is only natural
that the tedium of the mere goose-step
will very soon pall upon them and damp
their ardour. They have enlisted to fight
for their country. My advice is, do not let
them cool down; strike while the iron
is hot, give them food of interesting work
and not the dry bones of mechanical drill.
Drill has its uses for moving bodies of men

rapidly and in good order for manoeuvring purposes, but it is not the end-all of their training. The spirit which is inculcated into the men is of far greater importance.

Mere drill can only manufacture soldiers very slowly, and, where there is need for speeding-up the training, a certain amount of imagination and a great deal of go have to be employed by the officers carrying out the instruction, as well as by the men themselves in receiving it.

We have an illustration of this brought very vividly before us to-day in the respective fighting qualities of the Belgian and German soldier and their fitness to win. No one will deny that in drill and drill-book lore the German is far ahead of the Belgian; yet the *élan* and intelligence of the latter render him an equally good soldier. The newspapers are full of authenticated instances of small parties of Belgian or British soldiers consisting of a dozen or twenty men defeating much larger bodies of the enemy, and always because of individual initiative and the right spirit which constitutes fitness to win.

SUCCESS IN WAR

The *Training Regulations* for the British army lay down as a first item that "The sole object of military training is to prepare our forces for war, success in battle being constantly held in view as the ultimate aim."

The first point laid down in the Field Service Regulations is:

"*Success in war depends more on the moral than on the physical qualities*. Skill cannot compensate for want of courage, energy; and determination: but even high moral quality may not avail without careful preparation and skilful direction. *The development of moral qualities is therefore first of the objects to be attained*; the next are organisation and discipline which enable those qualities to be controlled and used when required."

These then are the foundations, or should be, of the training of the soldier. Were they always borne in mind by instructors of recruits the training would be more interesting, more effective, and more rapid; but it is almost traditional with us that the whole process of training should begin with the physical side, the drilling and the setting up, and, excellent though the manuals are and the principles which they express, still it is difficult for the young officer or non-commissioned officer to see from them exactly where he can bring in the moral attributes demanded, when training his squad in the accepted forms of barrack-square drill. Perhaps some of these hints may be a help to him.

### THE GERMAN EMPEROR ON OUR ALPHA-
### BETICAL METHODS

I once had the interesting experience of having a talk with the present German Emperor regarding the relative value of the different arms in the field; and His Majesty said, "You will observe that I put the infantry in the front line on parade, while the cavalry, artillery, engineers, and train come in the second line. The infantry take the place of honour, since, by virtue of their armament and action, it is the infantry who win the battles; the remainder are their servants." I cordially acquiesced in the Emperor's statement; but then he turned on me and put me a "poser," "Why, then, do you in England put the artillery in the place of honour on the right of the line, the cavalry next, and then the engineers, and lastly the infantry?" I was rather at a loss for an answer, and blurted out the first idea that came into my head. I said, "I suppose it is that we place them in alphabetical order," and this answer greatly pleased His Majesty, if one could judge by the chuckling which lasted for some time afterwards.

## II

### THE FOUR C'S OF SOLDIERING
#### 1.   COURAGE

WELL, if we do these things in alphabetical order, let us be consistent. There are other things besides drill which go to make the soldier. There are four very important attributes, so important that I need not touch on any others in these pages, and these all begin with the letter "C." Therefore in our training they should surely come before Drill, which commences with a "D." They are:

Courage, Common-sense, Cunning, Cheer-fulness.

#### THE DEVELOPMENT OF COURAGE

Some men are born brave, others require

to have it thrust upon them. But in the large majority of cases it is a quality which can be cultivated. Without it a soldier is practically useless in the field. I do not know that drill goes very far towards developing it. I believe that for a man gifted with ordinary bodily development and health it is largely the outcome of confidence in himself, in his leaders, and in his comrades. It may be remembered of General Grant that in the American War of North and South he admitted that in his first action he found himself in a desperate funk, and was dodging and creeping along behind cover in order to evade the enemy's aim, when he noticed that those who were out against him were doing precisely the same thing, and soon he realised that they were just as much afraid of him as he was of them. Buoyed with a new hope, he rushed at them, and they at once incontinently took to their heels. He never felt afraid again, but always pushed forward in the sure confidence that the bolder his advance the more rapid would be the retirement of the enemy. But this same confidence in self can only come where the man knows that he is at least equal to if not better than the enemy opposed to him.

### CONFIDENCE IN YOURSELF

If your man is an infantryman he must feel confident that he is able to march long distances without feeling the weight of his kit or suffering in his feet. He must know that he is expert with his rifle, and that not only is he a good shot at the target on the range, but that he is able to hit moving objects in the field, and, above all, is an accurate judge of distance.

These, then, must be some of the first objects of your training.

### MARKSMANSHIP

In South Africa we always had the idea that the Boers were first-class marksmen. I have on many occasions fired matches with them. On the fixed rifle-range at known distances they could not hold their own against soldier-marksmen, but in the field when firing at moving objects and having to estimate for himself the distance and the allowance to make for the speed of the target, the ordinary soldier could not hold a candle to the Boers. It was that power of estimating distance in an atmosphere to which he was accustomed which gave the Boer his superiority.

The German Army instructions for judging distance are given as follows:

At 50 yards the mouth and eyes of the enemy can clearly be seen.

At 100 yards the eyes appear as dots.

At 200 yards buttons and details of uniform can still be seen.

At 300 yards faces can still be seen.

At 400 yards movement of the legs can be seen.

At 500 yards colour of the uniform can be seen.

## JUDGING DISTANCE

These are all very well when you can see your enemy in the field, but so often you can see nothing of him, and consequently have to judge by objects near to which he lies. Then it has to be remembered that these objects look much nearer when the light is bright and shining upon them, or when looking across water or snow, or looking up or down hill. Objects appear further off than they really are when in the shade, across a valley, when the background is of the same colour, when the observer is lying down or kneeling, or when there is a heat haze over the ground.

Judging distance has by practice to be a second habit with a man if he is to be a good shot in the field. In these days it has to include, in addition to its ordinary features, the estimation of heights at which an enemy's aeroplane is flying. The airman is not going to fly low if he sees troops waiting for him. You have got to learn how to hide from him and to ambush hostile aircraft, and not to fire without a good chance of bringing him down, otherwise he will from your firing gain the information he desires as to your whereabouts.

When you are firing at aircraft, don't forget that your bullets or shells have got to come down again after meeting the flyer. Whom are you likely to damage thus?

### CONFIDENCE IN YOUR HORSEMANSHIP

Another kind of confidence needed in our soldiers is that of being able to act alone in the darkness at night. With a little practice it is wonderful what a difference it makes to a man's capabilities for useful work.

If our soldier belongs to the mounted branch he can have little confidence in himself if he is not a good horseman and mounted on a good horse. By horseman I do not mean that he is able to ride and handle his horse under the many situations required of a cavalry soldier, but that he is also an efficient horse-master, and knows how to keep his horse fit for action and capable of a life-ride at any moment. These are matters which come only by training and practice, and which no amount of drill will inculcate.

### CONFIDENCE IN YOUR PALS

Yet another step to confidence is that of knowing that his comrades around him are all equally good men; that they understand their job, and will play the game and stick it out with him to the end. This they can only do by knowing what the game is, having an intelligent interest in it, and having a certain amount of sense of self-sacrifice and helpfulness to each other in getting the work done. The spirit in the men is of greater value than any other quality that. can be produced. It is, in fact, another "C", viz., that of character which goes to make them efficient for war. Now, this character and spirit are about the last things that drill will put into a man, yet of all things they are the most valuable.

### CONFIDENCE IN YOUR LEADERS

The last form of confidence, which is possibly the most important of them all for giving a man courage in the field, is confidence in his leader. To inspire confidence in his men the leader must as a matter of course have absolute confidence in himself. He can only have this if he knows the whole of his work from A to Z, and if he feels that he is ready to meet any occasion or any tricks that Fate may try to play on him in the strenuous work of active service. His men are observing him all the time, they are quick to read his character, because instinctively they feel that their lives are largely in his hands. They are quick to detect any nervousness or hesitation in his action and to adopt it as their own, but they are even more quick, fortunately for us, to catch on to any dash and bravery and self-confidence which he may display. If he possesses that electric touch of leadership which comes from the possession of the four "C's" of soldiering, they will brace their minds and follow him if need be to the gates of hell.

### MACHINE-MADE DISCIPLINE

That is the secret of discipline. The so-called military discipline of repression by punishment for any neglect of orders is a soul-destroying machine which strangles true efficiency. The old iron-bound discipline of former days which regulated more brutish minds to the hand of brave and manly, though it may be unintelligent officers, has given place to a higher tone of discipline which comes of a sense of playing the game for one's side, and of carrying out a difficult or dangerous task from a sense of duty rather than from fear of punishment. This, if it is coupled with a genuine belief in the powers of the leader, constitutes the highest and most enthusiastic form of discipline, such as carries men through tight places and wins battles.

Among the many duties laid down for an officer there is one which I have not seen prominently alluded to, and yet it has a very important bearing on the confidence of the men in themselves and in their ability to carry out an arduous campaign, and is therefore an important step towards courage. Those who have not been on active service scarcely realise the change of atmosphere which comes over the men after a few days or weeks of campaigning. The average spectator only sees the men going on service like lions, and is unaware of what lambs they become when worn with marching, "fed up," as they call it, with hard fare and hardships. Thus the health and fitness of the men is really a matter of extreme importance; and just as the cavalryman should be a good horse-master as well as a good horseman, the commander of troops must be a good man-master as well as a good man-leader in the field.

### HEALTH AS A STEP TO COURAGE

"It is just as much part of the soldier's duty to be healthy as to be a good horseman or a good shot; and it is just as much the duty of the officer to teach him how to be so and to see that he is so as to teach him to ride or to shoot or to be efficient in other ways." This was a warning which I once had to publish on the subject of sickness. In the South African campaign we had 18,000 men admitted to hospital for wounds, but nearly 400,000 for sickness, though South Africa is not such a very unhealthy country.

The average men do not know how to look after their own personal hygiene in the slightest degree, and officers will do well to impress upon them a few useful hints in the course of their training for war. Drill will not do it.

### HOW TO INCULCATE COURAGE

Above all, the officer must include in his scheme of training the teaching of the spirit and moral of soldiering. To the importance of this I have already drawn attention. I will here add a few suggestions towards its development in the men. Whether you are an officer or N.C.O. teaching, or a man learning, courage, practise these points which make you an expert at your work as a fighting-man. You will gain confidence in yourself as being at least as good, if not better, than your opponent, whether at

Marching,
Judging distance,
Straight shooting,
Horsemanship,
Scouting,

Stalking,

Night work,

Entrenching,

Skill with bayonet, sword, or lance. These come by practice and competition more quickly than by drill. General Nogi, the great Japanese leader who displayed in his life and in his death the highest personal courage, said that though timid by nature he had developed this quality by stern self-discipline. When he found a job which caused him apprehension or fear he forced himself to face it, and to repeat it again and again until it no longer had any terrors for him. It is that taking oneself firmly in hand that enables a man to stick it out against the impulse of his knees to give in or to run away in a crisis.

### THE GERMAN EMPEROR ON ATTACK

Confidence—the component of courage—comes also from the knowledge that you are not recklessly being sacrificed. I once had a little argument on this point with the German Emperor. He objected to the system in our training which teaches the men to spread out and to take cover in advancing to the attack. He said, "You teach them to be afraid of the bullets before they have even heard one. In the German Army we march the men by rank after rank of their fellows; they cannot fail to carry the position."

This seems a good theory, but one wants to see the result before one can judge. I imagine it would require an army very strong in reserves and very strong in nerves to carry it through successfully. Our army is small and we cannot supply the weight of numbers required for this form of confidence.

The more intelligent the men the less inclination they have to be ruthlessly sacrificed; and their confidence will be increased as they see their leader has discretion and only takes risks that are reasonable.

### SAVING YOUR MEN

One of my best officers showed great aptitude in saving his men when moving under fire. At all times they moved as if being shot at, keeping close to the sides of the roads, advancing by short rushes and then lying flat. It thus became a second nature to them to arrive at the spot needed very rapidly, unseen by the enemy and without casualties in their ranks. When it came to charging in with the bayonet they were all there, and did not mind what losses they suffered; and their leader, coupled with his discretion, was the bravest officer I have ever met.

One officer earned the name among his men of "Back-door P—," because when he led them into a nasty place he generally

explained to them that he had an alternative way out of it again, and this gave
them no end of confidence.

Discretion therefore need not be confused
with funk, unless carried to that excess
which stamps it as such.

# III

## THE FOUR C'S OF SOLDIERING

### 2. COMMON-SENSE

THE science of strategy and the art of tactics look formidable when contained between the covers of many volumes, and yet they are, after all, nothing more than the application of common-sense to the situation. Strategical moves are those of the chess-player in putting out his pieces where they will stand to the best advantage for carrying out the game of war when it comes to hand-grips, or tactics; that is, the operations and movements of the troops in actual contact with each other. The books lay down definite principles and examples which serve to guide the leaders when applying their common-sense to the situation before them. No two situations are ever precisely the same, and it is therefore impossible to lay down exact rules that should guide in every case, but a man who carries precedents and principles in his head has no difficulty in applying their teachings in supreme moments of sudden emergency.

For quick training it is, however, essential that a man should understand that the book rules are not necessarily to be followed to the letter, although the principle remains essential. He must apply his own common-sense, and apply it in the simplest possible form if he wishes to be successful.

### THE TRIANGULAR FORMATION

In the soldier's phrase, "a pound of fresh is worth a ton of bully," and perhaps a little drop of experience by one who has tried it may be worth a bucketful of regulations. I have found it simplest for quick training and have never found it fail in war, the principle of having one's

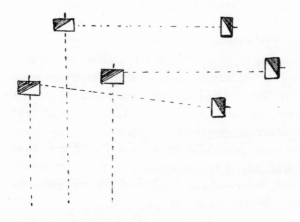

A force marching in Triangle is suddenly required to meet an attack to its right. The body nearest the enemy becomes the front line. The remainder conform and become support and reserve respectively.

force disposed in triangular fashion. I would not lay this down as a fetish that is always to be adhered to, but I mention it as a useful formation when in doubt.

It is a simple proposition and a common-sense one, whether your force is a moving one, or a halted one, or a fixed one, and it applies whether your force is an army corps or a division, a regiment or a patrol. In moving over open country, whether expecting an enemy or not, it is easier to go with one body leading and two others on its exposed and protected rear in support and reserve respectively. I have generally gone against propositions which lay down that such and such a direction is your front, and have always treated every side as my front. Thus, if your moving triangle be attacked from an unexpected quarter it makes no difference to your safety or your dispositions; the body nearest to the enemy becomes the front line and the remaining two become reserve and support respectively.

If your force is halted it can often be better halted in three separate parties than

in one massed camp. In this way there
can be no-surprise; if one camp is suddenly

Triangular formation as applied to a Patrol.

assailed the other two have time to get
under arms and to protect it.

The Triangular Formation may be
applied to a patrol of three men. If there

are more, they take position as numbered on the accompanying sketch in order of importance. The commander keeps near the centre to be in touch with all.

Similarly with a fixed force holding entrenchments, if these are disposed in three positions, mutually supporting each other, it is far more effective than if they are all placed in one big work.

### A TYPICAL CAVALRY FIGHT

Let me instance a typical cavalry fight as an example of what is meant by common-sense in tactics, and this use of the triangular formation. "The Southern division in column of route on the main road learnt that the enemy's division was about two miles distant to its left. Leaving the road, our division formed into preparatory formation with one brigade in front and two in the second line. Our scouts soon signalled that the enemy was in sight approaching the left front. Our guns came into action without delay on the enemy's main body,

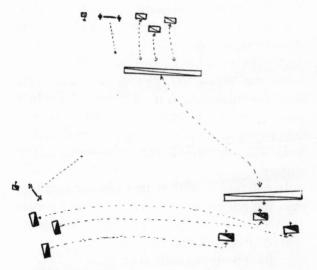

The Triangular Formation and the development of an attack.

while our division took ground to the right and thus drew the enemy on to attack it. Then the enemy formed line preparatory

to charging, but our division still kept on
its course across the front of the enemy
in preparatory formation, thus causing
him to alter his direction (which it was
almost impossible to do in good order when
committed to line), and *at the same time
drew him across the fire of our guns.* At
the last moment our division, wheeling
each brigade into line with its left, charged
the enemy in double echelon in good order,
and was accorded the victory by the
umpire."

It will be seen that in carrying out this
plan the enemy were not only drawn across
the front of our guns, but were also prevented from firing into our division by
their own body masking their guns.

### THE BOERS AT MAJUBA

How the Boers took Majuba Hill in 1881
has always been a useful lesson to me, and
I believe that its lesson is just as good for

fighting to-day, whether for a big or a little action. It was again an instance of common-sense tactics, and especially it showed the value of "covering fire." The British force was on the summit of a high, steep-

The attack on Majuba.

sided mountain which overlooked everything. The older Boers took position on a neighbouring hilltop about half the height of Majuba and fired at anyone who looked over the crest of the mountain. The younger and more active Boers meantime climbed up the face of the mountain, without being observed or fired upon until they had collected together immediately under the crest, over which no British soldier could show a nose on account of the covering fire from the neighbouring hill. Thus the attackers were able to rush the defenders.

### THE IMPORTANCE OF COVERING FIRE

I have seldom seen an attack where covering fire from a separate body told off for the purpose was not of the highest value. I am talking now of small actions, for in the larger ones artillery would naturally do the preparation and covering fire to a great extent. It is, however, surprising how often a commander neglects or probably forgets to make use of it, and finds his task of attacking all the more difficult in consequence; yet it is only a matter of common-sense. Therefore I commend the habitual use of covering-fire at all minor tactical exercises.

### THE COMMON SENSE USE OF CAVALRY

If cavalry are cunning they will feed their horses and rest themselves all the morning, and, like the well-known General in South Africa, will "put off rounding up the enemy till after luncheon."

Why?

Because the opportunity for the cavalry comes when the enemy's infantry have had a bellyful of marching and fighting all day and have run short of ammunition, and are weak for want of food. It may be unkind, but that is the time to go for them.

### TRENCHES AND DEFENCE WORKS

Trenches and defence works come very much into modern tactics, and here again common-sense is the best director of field engineering: In South Africa we employed what were termed C. S. trenches, that is,

Common Sense trenches, whose plan generally took the form of a C or an S.

These trenches again had no special front; they were prepared for attack in any direction; they were low and narrow, and thus offered no target for artillery and gave complete cover from shot, shell, and weather to their garrison. They were many times attacked during the campaign, but in no single instance were they ever taken. They were constructed in this way. Each man of the garrison had a task assigned him of six feet by three to excavate to a depth of three feet, piling up the earth on either side of him. A roof of corrugated iron covered with earth was erected over this, and long, low loopholes were made along both sides. These loopholes again were of common-sense order, that is to say, they were two feet wide by two inches high. instead of the usual two inches wide and four inches high. By this means the

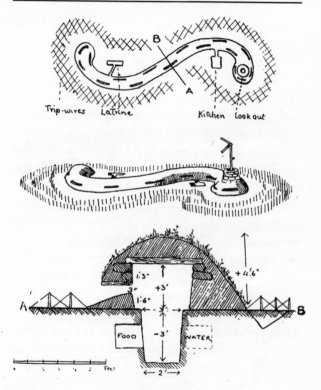

1. Plan.  2. Elevation.  3. Section.
The Common Sense Trench.

defenders had a wide range of view at no greater risk from dropping bullets, while with the ordinary narrow loophole a man's view was very limited and his power of elevating his rifle very great: the consequence was that on more than one occasion a kind of panic seized the men holding a fort or block-house equipped with the upright loopholes. They could see nothing to fire at immediately opposite them, but hearing their right and left neighbours firing away, they were seized with an insane desire to loose off also. They did so, and at any sort of elevation that came into their mind. Ammunition was wasted by the ton, and an enterprising enemy, had he come up to demand their surrender, would probably have got it through the giving out of their ammunition.

# LOOPHOLES

### 1. As they should be

Solid overhead

Long and low
sandbags or earth
fairly near ground

### 2. As they should not be

Slight over head

Narrow
stony wall

High above ground
and therefore a
target for artillery

Loopholes and how to make them.

### THE C.S. TRENCH

In the C. S. trenches, with their wide
loopholes, the men could see out in every
direction and thus had confidence. The
lowness of the loophole precluded the

Line of trenches open to enfilade by distant artillery or rifle
fire, or to be fired into from the rear.

A group of C. S. trenches free from these objections.

entrance of bullets fired at a long range,
and prevented the men from themselves
firing with high sights. Consequently they
had to carry out to the letter that maxim

which has led to success in many a great
defence: "Lie low and shoot straight."

They did what the Belgians have recently
done at Liége: they had to reserve their

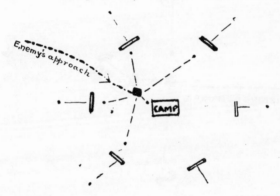

Protected camp—How not to do it. Trenches facing outwards :
The enemy enters between two and takes them all in the rear.

fire until the enemy was close up, but they
then opened with deadly accuracy at the
distance of a few yards with an effect
that there was no withstanding, and the
enemy had to beat a retreat under the full

force of their musketry. These loopholes
had a further advantage of giving room for
more than one man to fire from them

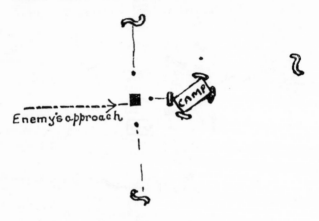

Protected camp. The common-sense way, the trenches facing
all ways. The enemy enters and is under cross fire.

when heavy fire was required at any one
point; and also being placed close to the
ground level, they were almost as deadly
at night as they were in the day, since they

gave the firers no chance of aiming over the attackers' heads.

The following sketches show the effect of

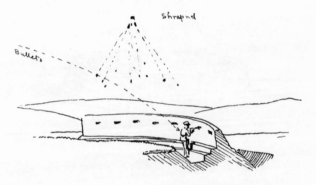

A very usual work, but open to aeroplane bombs, shrapnel, and bullets in reverse.

shrapnel, bullets, and aeroplane bombs upon defensive works, and illustrate the advantage of even an unfinished C. S. trench.

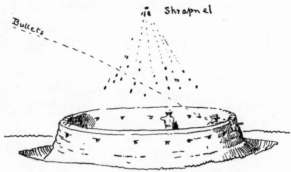

A very usual work also open to aeroplane bombs, shrapnel, and bullets
in reverse.

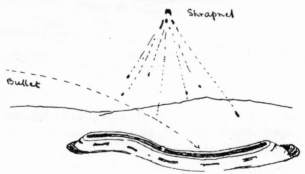

A C. S. trench in a half-completed state, but comparatively safe.

### SAND-BAG DEFENCES

Another common-sense way of making a work or shelter where the nature of the soil or other reasons prevent digging is with sand-bags, and I have seen it done with surprising effect by the Boers in South Africa. The site for a work may be decided upon during daylight where the ground is too much exposed to view or fire to be immediately occupied, but under the cover of darkness a party of men equipped with a dozen sand-bags apiece and a small spade or trowel can go to the spot, and with a few minutes of work can build up a sufficiently strong earth-work to protect them at all events from rifle-fire. Lodgments can be made in this way even in carrying out the attack on a force in position.

To be able to rush from point to point, taking advantage of cover and losing few

men, and then being able to entrench
themselves in such works as these, is of
more value than being able to march in well-
ordered columns to be mowed down
in attacking a position; and yet the
training for able-bodied men with reasonable intelligence would take far less time
than the drill required for the manoeuvring.
A little training in pick and shovel work
and in pioneering is easily acquired; it
interests the men and may be of first
importance on service.

### COMMON-SENSE DODGINESS

What immense labour is involved in
digging communication trenches between
outlying works in a defence! When we
had worn out our backs and tools in making
these at Mafeking we found we could get
just as effective cover from view by running
up a few strips, of canvas on stakes, behind
which the men could pass to and fro unseen

by the enemy—except when the sun set behind them, when they made a shadow-pantomime upon the screen!

Sentries are taught in theory to march up and down their post and to challenge all comers in a loud, clear voice. But in practice common-sense tells them that this is about the last way they should carry out their duty on service. There their system, instead of giving away their position to a watchful scout, is to lie low near the probable path of anyone approaching, and to whisper a hoarse, "Hands up!" in his ear, while "persuading" him with the point of a bayonet in his stomach!

The very best book from which to teach minor tactics in the defence of a post is *The Defence of Duffer's Drift*. You can read it to your men and they will be delighted and interested in its amusing series of very practical lessons in war.

### BRIDGING RIVERS

Common-sense teaches one that there are many ways of bridging rivers besides those laid down in hand-books, and that in countries intersected by water-cuts and canals with boggy bottoms it is essential that the men should be able to make their own means of passing such obstacles without waiting for professional engineers to come along and take measurements and work out plans and estimates before putting up an erection to carry them over.

### COMFORT IN CAMP

In camp the men should by practice have become experts in making themselves comfortable and therefore the more healthy under small but weatherproof shelters formed from materials to be found on the spot; and every man would be the happier and better if he could cook his own little meal when and where it suited him instead of having to go fasting for hours until the battalion cooks had got all their paraphernalia in order and the joints and vegetables cooked in the orthodox manner. The old soldier who carries his "billy" filled with the scraps from the last meal and merely has to heat it up on a little fire at a convenient halt is the envy of all his comrades, and is the healthiest and cheeriest among them.

### GIVING ORDERS CLEARLY

In the matter of giving orders a depth of importance lies in their being given concisely and with the utmost clearness. If the men really understand their instructions they can carry them out with all the greater effectiveness, and if the officer can only remember to give the reasons for his orders, as well as the bald orders themselves, they will be carried out with far greater spirit and energy because the men understand and are in his confidence.

### CONCEALMENT

Concealment of the presence of troops is often of the greatest value in war, and is easier than may be imagined if every man is trained to the job. Hostile scouts, or aeroplanes, may suddenly appear and have a look over your position, and even a large force, dressed as we are in khaki, can often escape detection if it observes the common rules for hiding. These are given in *Aids to Scouting*, and generally consist in choice of background to suit the colour of your clothes, "freezing," i.e., standing still as a statue until the observer has passed, dulling or shadowing all bright accoutrements, rifle-barrels, etc., likely to catch the eye. This is a matter for practice. From an aeroplane it is very difficult to distinguish large bodies of troops on roads, provided that the roads are damp and not sending up clouds of dust, and provided that the march discipline of the troops is good—that is, that they are in well closed up bodies and keeping well together along one side of the road, so as to look like a brown path alongside the white road.

### HOW TO INCULCATE COMMON-SENSE

As a step to inculcating common-sense I should give definite responsibility to every N.C.O. down to the corporal in charge of a squad: let him have that squad as his permanent unit for whose smartness and efficiency he alone is answerable; and let him have all the praise or the blame according to the standard that it attains.

With emulation between the several squads the standard of the whole rises by leaps and bounds.

When commanding the constabulary in South Africa I was given the duty of escorting Joseph Chamberlain on his tour through the country. At one point of our journey we saw a solitary trooper of the force riding across the veldt. Mr. Chamberlain asked me what would be this man's duty. I replied that as a rule police patrols went about their districts in pairs; when a man was not sufficiently intelligent or self-reliant he was sent alone on long journeys in order to cultivate and develop his common-sense and self-reliance. On signalling the man to us on this occasion a few questions showed that he was going through such form of self-education.

Develop the intelligence of the individuals and the whole unit will be efficient.

Deduction of the meaning of small signs is a step towards developing common-sense, and this has to start with practice in observation and noticing such signs before putting them together to find their meaning.

A very effective step to this end, since

its interest grows upon the pupils, is the art of tracking and reading signs, the details of which I have gone into more fully in *Aids to Scouting*.

Then night scouting and night outposts, night attacks and night field-firing, develop the faculties far more quickly than the same practices carried out by day, and are of real, practical value for efficiency on service.

I once had to ride some thirty miles with despatches through an enemy's country. I did it in the night, guiding myself by the stars, and on arriving where I thought the Headquarter Camp ought to be I failed to find it. I was beginning to think that I should have to wait for dawn to discover it, when I noticed what appeared to be the gleam of a distant camp-fire. I walked eagerly towards it, when I suddenly bumped into a sentry smoking his pipe. It was the glare of this which had deceived me, but it had guided me. I was too grateful to run the man in for his want of common-sense in thus giving away his position to a watchful enemy.

## IV

### THE FOUR C'S OF SOLDIERING

#### 3. CUNNING

IMAGINATION is an invaluable factor in conducting warfare. The commander has naturally to picture to himself the many situations that might arise, and to decide how he would deal with them. He is in this way prepared for all emergencies, but he has to go further and imagine to himself the ideas that are guiding his enemy, and then to find a plan with which to outwit him. This was one of the secrets of Napoleon's success. When his intelligence officers had ascertained for him the disposition of his enemy, knowing to a T the character of his opposing general, he would figure to himself what his plan of action was likely to be. He would then formulate a plan of his own for counteracting it, and, in the event of this not being entirely practicable, he would make a second alternative plan; either of these plans might be practicable on account of their conformation with the accepted tactical or strategical principles. Then Napoleon would bring his imagination into play and devise yet a third scheme—such as would not probably have been foreseen by his opponent; and this was the one which preferably he would play upon him.

WHERE CUNNING SCORES

That is where cunning comes in. For quick training in cunning, the best school is that of Scouting. The first steps in making a good scout are to teach him Observation and Deduction, noticing every detail about the enemy, and deducing a meaning from the points observed. Then

by a little imagination the enemy's move-
merits or intentions are read, and counteracting steps can be taken with every
advantage.

One could easily write a complete book—
and it has indeed already been done—on
cunning in war;* and though many of
the ideas may be classed as playing the
fool, there is no doubt that certain armies
or leaders suffer from a lack of imagination
which is almost fatal to successful work.
A little example which occurred at
manoeuvres will suffice to explain my
meaning.

An officer in charge of a cavalry squadron
reconnoitring the enemy observed a hostile
battery in action behind the crest of a very
steep bank, while its cavalry escort was
some distance away to a flank keeping
guard over it. He saw that if he could
approach from the unprotected flank and

* See Col. Malleson's *Ruses and Stratagems of War*.

get close, under the front of the battery, screened by the bank he could probably rush it. This manoeuvre he carried out with complete success. On comparing notes at the subsequent pow-wow the officer who had been guarding the battery said that he had been misled by the dryness of the country into thinking that the dust of hostile cavalry would give him ample warning of their coming. The next day this battery again was in action, with its cavalry commander evidently again on the look-out for dust. So the attacking leader readily obliged him by sending off three or four men down a lane to his immediate front towing behind them large branches of trees, which raised a splendid cloud of dust as they went along. Away went the dashing commander on their trail, and charging into the dust found himself a captor of a number of branches and three or four men, while in the meantime the main body of his opponent's cavalry had walked into his battery and again captured it.

## OUT-BOERING THE BOER

At Mafeking, by constantly studying with our glasses, we ascertained that the enemy's works were surrounded by wire entanglements. On Sundays there was no firing between the forts, and the garrisons accordingly came outside to stretch their legs. We knew that the wire entanglements were there from seeing how the men stepped over some of the wires and crawled under others. We therefore put up wire entanglements round our works also, in order to discourage the enemy from attacking them. But we anticipated science by making our entanglements "wireless," for we had not sufficient material in the place to make them of real wire. We planted upright stakes in great numbers and the men were instructed when coming out or entering a fort to do a good deal of stepping high and crawling low for the information of enemies who might be watching through their glasses. Their newspaper accounts of the siege enlarged upon the impossibility of taking our works owing to entanglements.

### MASTERS OF CUNNING

It is perhaps difficult to say where common-sense ends and cunning begins, but both are required for successful tactics. The Boers were remarkably clever in hiding their field guns, so that they were able to shell us for a considerable time before we could locate the position of their artillery sufficiently well to reply to it effectively. Thus they did not carry out the usual rule given in our books of instructions, viz., of clearing the front of their position of all bush, etc., but preferred to keep the natural plants standing in front of them, so long as they got a sufficient aperture for aligning their sights on their object. With smokeless powder, and with the flash of the guns thus screened, our only way of locating them was to notice where the dust caused by the shock of discharge rose in the air; but this the Boers got over in a way which might be attributed either to common-sense or cunning: they used to carry ox-hides rolled up on their limbers, and these they spread on the ground beneath the muzzles of the guns before firing, and thus prevented the dust being kicked up.

The Boers also made it a practice in selecting sites for their guns or for rifle trenches to put them in most unexpected positions. Thus in attacking a strong looking hill which you would expect to find crowned with trenches and with artillery concealed over the crest, you probably discovered after much waste of ammunition that the defenders were entrenched at the foot of the hill with their guns half-way up it, and generally with some clever line of retreat in a fold or ravine through which they could withdraw unseen.

### HOW TO INCULCATE CUNNING

The art of hiding, whether behind a screen or in front of a background of the right colour, is taught in scouting and is a fascinating study as well as an invaluable accomplishment for a soldier. In *Aids to Scouting* I have given a number of games and competitions which tend to develop cunning in war.

I remember being caught out when inspecting the scouts of a certain cavalry regiment. I stood on a central knoll and sent out the scouts each in a different direction to creep unseen towards me and then to watch all that I did and note it down. Meantime I should keep a look-out and should set a mark against each man whom I detected watching or moving. At the end of the exercise I called them all in, examined their reports, and then deducted marks from those whom I had spotted. One man had done an excellent report, but I told him that with much regret I had seen him about five times peering at me through the bushes; he ought to have used more cunning. Then he explained that he had found a countryman near where he was hiding, so he had told him to look very cautiously and he would see me do some very funny tricks, but he must not let himself be seen or I should probably not perform. It was the decoy whom I had seen. I had no reason to blame the scout for want of cunning!

### RUSES OF WAR

A scouting officer in the South African campaign saved himself from being captured by exercising his bump of cunning. He had crept out along a dry watercourse to reconnoitre a Boer fort, and he knew that when he got back to a certain bush which grew over the bank he would be pretty close up to the work and in a position to study it. He came to the bush all right and put his head up, but could see no sign of the fort to his front. He raised himself higher to have a better look, and suddenly heard a sound behind him. Glancing round he found that he had passed the bush for which he had been aiming; it stood some few feet back from the bank instead of on it, and he had gone on to a second bush. In doing so he had passed the fort. The noise that he had heard was caused by some of the Boers who had been sitting in the rear of the work and who had seen him rise up out of the ditch. They were now all alert and moving as if to capture him. In a moment he turned round as if to a crowd of men behind him in the ditch and signalled with the greatest energy to them to lie down and keep hidden, and then slid down himself, as if to join them below the bank. But as he went he had the satisfaction of seeing the Boers scuttling as hard as they could go for the shelter of the fort, only dreading lest a volley should catch them before they got there!

Another scouting officer, riding up apparently rather blindly towards a batch of the enemy, had to turn and gallop for his life. As he did so he *accidentally* dropped his map. On this was marked the route which his main body was to take that day, with some notes as to its intentions—all of it valuable information to the enemy if it had been true; but it was not. But it took in their leaders and sent them on a wild-goose chase.

The Boers were cunning in their actions, but were of all people the most easily taken in by cunning. Don't let that be your fate.

# V

## THE FOUR C'S OF SOLDIERING

### 4.  CHEERFULNESS

I HAVE said before that the spirit which possesses the men is a tremendous factor for success in war, and the presence of a few infallibly cheerful men in the ranks, and more especially among the leaders, is of a value that cannot be over-estimated in an arduous campaign or when things are going against you. Anyone who has played football, polo, or cricket, or indeed has taken part in any team work, knows well the value of a captain who can face the worst of games with a cheery smile, how it puts heart into all, and inspires them to buck up and do their best, even though things may be looking hopeless.

It is just the same in war. And it must be remembered that war is not what the picture-books would have us believe—a continuous succession of glorious battles, but it is much more like the experiences described by Emile Zola in *Le Débâcle*, viz., a dreary succession of days and weeks of hard and apparently aimless marching, dull, dreary tramping in great herds, under heavy loads, utterly fagged and weary, without excitement, without hope, one's only thoughts centred on how to get a meal; that utter weariness of body and soul which make men quite resigned to being shot. An army in this state is already half-way to defeat, were it not that its opponents are probably in much the same state. But here it is that a few cheery spirits exercise a vitalising influence and are worth the presence of hundreds of extra men to their force.

### A FACTOR IN SUCCESS

I have known of more than one officer who was accepted for service, not so much on account of his military ability as for his undampable spirits, which invariably develop a brighter feeling among those around him. A commander will therefore do well to cultivate in himself and in those around him a cheery spirit of optimism and an energetic activity in carrying out all orders conveyed to him. His example will be contagious. The officer who is ready to obey orders will find his men equally active in carrying out his own. It often needs a power of self-discipline on the part of the leader not to show anxiety when anxiety would be justifiable; but to show courage and fortitude with a smiling face even in the most hopeless and depressing circumstances is a God-sent gift. As stated in *Scouting for Boys*,

"If you are in the habit of taking things cheerfully you will very seldom find yourself in serious trouble, because if a difficulty or annoyance or danger seem very great, you will if you are wise force yourself to laugh at it—although I will allow it is very difficult to do so at first. Still, the moment you do laugh most of the difficulty seems to disappear at once and you can tackle it quite easily. Bad language and swearing are often used to cover loss of self-control. Generally a man who swears the loudest is the man most easily upset, and therefore loses his head in a difficult situation. He gets fussy and anxious and upsets everyone else. You want to be quite undisturbed under the greatest difficulties, and so when you find yourself particularly anxious or excited or angry, don't swear, but force yourself to smile and to whistle a little tune, and it will set you right in a moment."

But in advocating cheery optimism I

would not have you disregard danger or underestimate your enemy. Another scout's motto which may well be digested in this connection is that which, says, "See the worst, but look at the best side."

In the Boer War an officer was out reconnoitring with his troop when he came upon a couple of Boer farms with their outbuildings clustered together in a hollow among some rocks and bush. The scouts reported that a number of women and children were there, but no men. The women were quite friendly and came out and talked to them and invited the troops to have some coffee. Being of a genial and jovial nature the captain at once accepted, the troop were dismounted, and the women said they would run on to the house and get coffee ready. As soon as they had started and had got well away from the troop a sudden fire was opened on the men by a number of Boers hidden

in the neighbouring rocks. For a moment
the men were startled and inclined to lose
their heads in a panic, when the roaring
laughter of their captain was heard: he
thought the trap in which they had been
caught the funniest thing he had heard of
for a long time, and his cheery sangfroid
at such a moment at once brought back
their wits, and in a very few minutes they
had gone coolly to their work and had the
Boers out of their hiding-places and the
farm in flames.

### HOW TO INCULCATE CHEERFULNESS

However sad a dog you may be you have
got to cultivate a cheery spirit yourself
if you want those around you to have it
also. It is of the utmost importance to
yourself and the country that the men
should exercise a cheery optimistic feeling
in carrying on their work. They must not
be allowed to display anxiety or hysterics

under conditions that may cause either depression or elation; but they must be taught to make the best of things and to practise a cheery spirit and a ready obedience to further orders. Good health is a great step towards cheerful endurance and alacrity in carrying out commands; so, as I have urged above, health among the men ought to be very strenuously cultivated. Therefore take every opportunity of teaching your men about personal hygiene, home and camp sanitation, and all the little dodges of making themselves comfortable and healthy in camp, with camp comforts and good cooking, etc.

As a hint to impressing care of self on the men and their responsibility for their own health, let me quote General Sir William Knox. He records an interesting lesson which he gave to his men in the matter of health.

"A battalion of young soldiers fresh

from England joined my command, and knowing how important it was to impress upon all youngsters, not only the value of their lives to the nation, but the dangers that they would incur if they neglected to obey the instructions and orders for hygiene and sanitation, I met them on their arrival by train. I marched them straight off to the cemetery and formed three sides of a square. In brief words I told them that I had much experience of the country and had worked out a guide for their welfare and sanitation in the field. These orders would be read to them later on in camp by their officers. Pointing to the cemetery, I said, 'There are seven hundred and fifty of your comrades there, not fifty of whom died of wounds. You are seven hundred and eighty strong, and you will all be there unless you obey my orders. I have enlarged the cemetery for the purpose. March off to camp!'

Some years afterwards one of the officers told me what an effect my words and illustration had produced, and how in his own company of one hundred and thirty men he lost in fifteen months only one."[*]
On service cheerfulness depends a good deal on physical fitness, and this means not only good health but also such points as ability to get rested by knowing your work in camp and getting it done quickly and well, and thereby getting rest; e.g. if you are told off to slack off the tent ropes on a wet night, you do it by digging a little hole for the foot of the pole instead of going out and loosing each separate rope; also in knowing the little dodges of campaigning that overcome what a greenhorn calls hardships, but what the old hand takes in serene comfort, even if it is only

[*] *The Flaw in our Armour*, by Major-Gen. Sir W. Knox, K.C.B. With an Introduction by Field-Marshal Earl Roberts, V.C, K.G. 1s. net.

to dig the little hole for your hip-bone to rest in, which makes all the difference to your comfort when sleeping on the hard ground.

The ability to manage your feet and foot-gear is all-important to know: that corns come from beer as much as from bad boots; changing into shoes occasionally on the march gives great relief; a wrapping or "duffle" of soft rag round the foot inside the sock prevents many a sore foot. If you have to carry a water-bottle, carry it empty—every single ounce of weight tells on you, and every sip of water makes you less fit, while swills of it give you all the internal complaints you ever heard of.

## VI

### HOW TO CARRY OUT YOUR TRAINING

IT is difficult to lay down a practical method by which an officer can directly cultivate and develop the moral attributes required; but, as pointed out in the manuals, they are of paramount importance. The boys of our nation are not trained in these matters in their schools, and it is largely left to them to develop their individual character according to their surroundings and environment. The whole raison d'etre of the Boy Scouts Movement is to develop character by direct and practical steps, and if these should be of any use as suggested to a military instructor he has only to refer to the handbook, *Scouting for Boys*, to see the game and practices by which they may be inculcated.

GENERAL SCHEME FOR TRAINING—PARADES

In the instruction of his men, the officer should bear in mind the possibilities underlying each step of the training, and should as far as possible make each parade short and sweet; that is, make every moment of it instructive and at the same time interesting to the men. As a first step he would do well before going on parade to prepare a little programme of what he proposes to do in the course of the morning, and to make his scheme as varied and interesting as possible. A certain amount of drill instruction will no doubt be necessary, but if he keeps in view the aim and object of his training, which is how to fight effectively in the field, he will find his training grow with greater rapidity and effect if he makes a point of having a fight of some sort towards the end of each day's work; and this should always be done by opposing forces, no matter how small they may be.

Let nothing escape your notice. Allow men to make their mistakes, and point them out when they have made them.

## HOW TO MAKE THE TRAINING PRACTICAL AND INTERESTING TO THE MEN

Delegate authority and responsibility to your non-commissioned officers. Make their sections and squads as far as possible into permanent units under their entire command.

Promote emulation between sections or units by pitting them against each other in competitions or combats.

Make your men take notice of details as they march to or from their field-day ground.

Give reasons for each point of drill, or of physical exercises, so that your men will carry them out with greater interest, and therefore with better results.

Opposing forces may be placed under command of non-commissioned officers with a distinct problem to carry out. One side should wear, as distinguishing mark, white cap-covers, or coloured rags hanging from both shoulder-straps, or bunches of leaves. One side may form a convoy of sick to get from and to certain places while the enemy are instructed to reconnoitre and attack the convoy if found. One party may be instructed to lie in ambush while the other is told to march to a certain spot and report upon it. One party may be detailed to hold a bridge-head or defile which the other can attack. One party may practise building a bridge on a model scale with broomsticks and cords, with outposts for its protection against the opposing force, which meantime has to search for and attack it before the bridge can be completed.

One force could entrench itself and the other could attack when in position, using covering fire and hastily dug trenches. It is not always possible to dig earth and fill your sandbags, but a substitute, such

(1). How it was done in one case. The enemy were thus left to assemble on "dead" ground.

as grass, twigs, or newspapers, etc., can be used instead. The sandbag should in any case be built up on the correct principles for cover and defence.

It is desirable to practise problems of how you would defend buildings, etc., in your neighbourhood with the materials available on the spot. It is all important on every occasion when you have made or designed a defensive work to practise an attack upon it and so ascertain its weak

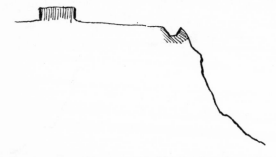

(2.) How it was done in two cases. The defenders showed up against the sky-line while the enemy were down the hollow in darkness.

points. The sketches I give here illustrate how to defend a house situated fifty yards from the edge of a cliff. It is assumed that the rear face is already protected.

It is always a useful practice at odd moments to fall out leaders and non-

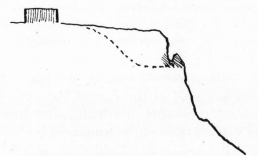

(3.) How it might have been done.

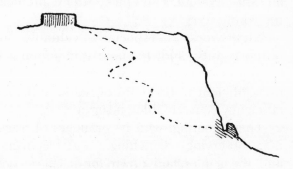

(4.) How the Boers would have done it.

commissioned officers as shot in action, and to let the next senior take their places without special orders to that effect. This should be practised almost every day. The officer acts as umpire at such tactical exercises, and at the end of the action he holds a pow-wow at which, after hearing the explanations of the leaders of both sides, he delivers judgment and criticism. Where the forces are small it is all the better if all ranks, N.C.O.'s and men, attend and hear the whole story.

Night-work is especially valuable for outpost duty and reconnaissance, etc. It is only practice and plenty of it that makes men efficient at this kind of work, and such efficiency is invaluable on service.

Then scouting, with its branches of track-ing, observing, sketching, and reporting, and the games laid down for its perfection in *Aids to Scouting*, is intensely interesting to men and offers a big programme of work.

In all of these the men take an interest and at the same time see the need of the different points of view, and pick them up almost automatically in half the time which it would take to teach them in the barrack-square.

### MINOR TRAINING SANDWICHED IN

The dull monotonous round of drill or the strenuous exertion of the field-day demand frequent halts and periods of rest. The doctors tell us that change of occupation is the best form of rest. Therefore these pauses, as well as the long waits on the ranges before it comes to a man's turn to fire, and the periods of inaction to which reserves and supports are condemned at field-days, should never be allowed to degenerate into waste of time. There are a thousand and one little things that soldiers want to know, and which the officers can well impart on such an occasion,

by way of change of occupation. Officers here have the power of turning what would otherwise be ennui and boredom into interesting progress and instruction. They can take the opportunity, for instance, of having distance-judging competitions on the objects around them.

They can:

Practise taking cover from aeroplanes, or from enemies.

Explain the various military ranks and their badges.

Medals and their ribbons.

The duties of despatch-riders and orderlies.

Practise semaphore or other signalling.

Bayonet or sword fighting.

Explain the latest war news and its lessons, both strategical and practicable.

Explain the map and teach map-reading.

How to read the stars for finding the way.

Explain the rules of war, as regards white flags, etc.

How wounded men are dealt with in action.

Prisoners of war, how taken and guarded.

Rules regarding flags of truce, and other such matters as described in the Field Service Regulations.

On these occasions encourage the men as much as possible to ask questions, as in that way you can discover very much in which direction their ignorance lies.

Play a tactical war game.

## TACTICAL WAR GAME

Once in an interval in a manoeuvre-fight I wanted to explain the tactical situation to some of my officers, so taking the summer horse-sheet which my groom had

thrown over my horse I spread it on the ground, and with stones and tufts of grass placed under it I made it into a rough model of the country we were working over. The sheet had a check pattern of squares of about two and a half to three inches across. These I used as quarter-mile squares. Stones of different sizes and colours represented the different bodies of troops, and opposing forces were moved from point to point on the ground with due regard to the time that it would take them to get there according to the scale.

The whole thing became so clear and so instructive that we afterwards elaborated it, and used it as an after-dinner game on a large table in the mess. A cardboard screen was slung across the centre of the table and rested with its lower edges upon it in order to hide the dispositions of the two forces from the opposing leaders until their reconnoitring parties had reached

points where they would actually be able to glean information. The screen was then raised by the umpires an inch or two, so that the leaders could peer underneath it and see as much of the enemy as the hills and woods, etc., in the opponent's country would allow, until they came in full view and the screen was raised.

The game became very realistic and most instructive to everybody. I learnt many tactical ideas and dodges from it myself.

It differed from the more elaborate war games in being tactical and not strategical and very simple in its rules and equipment.

You can teach your N.C.O.'s more in an hour at this game than you could in three or four days of manoeuvring, and in four or five years of barrack-square drill, and it develops their interest enormously.

### THE ATTITUDE OF THE OFFICER

In Santiago, Chili, there is a splendid statue of O'Higgins, the great Irish General who led the nation in its War of Independence. I describe the statue as "splendid" because it just typifies the man. Round the pedestal are engraved four of his famous sayings. One of these gives the key to the secret of his success in commanding the enthusiastic obedience of that wild people, although a foreigner himself.

"Come on, boys, to Death or Glory!"

He was pushing troops on to the attack, and had intended to say, "Go on, boys!" but his Spanish was not quite up to the mark, and one of his staff pointed out to him that he had used the word "Come" instead of "Go." "If I said 'Come on, boys,' I mean it," and he at once dashed to the head of the troops and led the charge. But in that little incident lies a heap of meaning to every officer and N.C.O. Never ask your men to do a thing you will not do yourself. Obedience to an order will often depend on how the order is put, and disobedience or a slack performance often originates in the nagging or sharp way in which the duty has been put upon the men. "Come on, lads, here's a job for us to do," is very different from, "Here, you! just you tackle that job, will you, or I'll know the reason why."

### VERBAL ORDERS

In giving orders to your subordinate, tell him clearly what you want done, but not necessarily how he is to do it. He can, especially if he be at some distance, judge better how to carry it into effect according to the circumstances on the spot. Besides, it is well to give initiative, discretion, and responsibility as a step to developing efficiency.

Verbal messages as carried by excited and untrained orderlies often create a great amount of confusion and loss of time and temper; in fact, they are great fun to the onlooker. In order to avoid this among your pupils it is well to give them practice at taking a verbal message and passing it on from man to man stationed at intervals in a wide circle. To make it more hurried and realistic, it can be done in competition by arranging two circles of relays and starting the same message simultaneously round each of them, to see which gets in most in the shortest time and most correctly.

I have not here touched on any of the technical details of drill or manoeuvre. These are to be found in the Military Manuals issued by authority. I have only indicated a few methods by which their teaching may be enhanced; but I firmly believe in making the training interesting to the men, so that they are encouraged to learn for themselves out of their own keenness, and the work thus becomes a form of self-*education* with them, instead of having the dry bones of *instruction* inflicted upon them.

### CONCLUSION

From some experience of training recruits and young soldiers under pressure of time I know the inestimable advantage of getting the right spirit into them as a groundwork on which to build their training. Too much drill at an early stage of their career is very apt to drive out every spark of this spirit. Therefore I commend the principle of giving them work that really interests them from the very first, and especially *at* the very first, the main effort being directed to making them intelligent and active campaigners, resourceful and self-reliant, very much as the Boers were owing to their home training and surroundings. After this train them in body and mind to their duty, and when they see better the reason for it, accurate drill and smartness can be added as a polish to the whole. Teach them from the first that they are like bricks in a wall, or players in a football team: each has to be perfect and efficient, each has to adhere patiently to the rules and to play in his place and to play the game—not for his own advancement or glorification, but simply and solely that at all costs his side may win.

THE END